Sales 101

Simple Solutions for Sales Success

by Shelley Kaehr, Ph.D.

FIRST EDITION
First Printing, 2007

Library of Congress Control Number:
Kaehr, Shelley A.—
          Sales 101: Simple Solutions for Sales Success /
Shelley Kaehr, Ph.D.—1st ed.

          c.   cm.
          ISBN: 9780964820951
          Library of Congress Control Number: 2007923460

Acknowledgements

To Tom Hopkins, for being an incredible example of what it means to rise to the top of the sales profession.

To Ray Last, for giving me the opportunity of a lifetime.

To Judy Slack, for her belief, vision & leadership.

To Linnea Armstrong, for lifelong friendship.

To Dr. Tammy Ledbetter, who encouraged me in this project from the beginning.

To Lee Compton, in memoriam, for being a shining example of a sales professional.

To my family, Mickey, Gail, and Mark, for supporting me through the years.

I am deeply grateful for the role each of you has played in my life. Thank You!

Contents

Introduction 6

One ◆ Rejoicing in the Title of Salesperson 10

Two ◆ Do What it Takes to Succeed 17

Three ◆ The Energy of Money 22

Four ◆ Get Motivated 32

Five ◆ Do As I Do 39

Six ◆ Product Knowledge 47

Seven ◆ You Are Your Company 52

Eight ◆ Types of Selling 59

Nine ◆ Detective Work: Features & Benefits 68

Ten ◆ Treasure Hunting: Finding People to Sell 74

Eleven ◆ Pipeline for Success 82

Twelve ◆ Qualifying 88

Thirteen ◆ Presentation 95

Fourteen ◆ Overcoming Obstacles/Objections 101

Fifteen ◆ Closing: The Art of Asking 111

Sixteen ◆ Referrals 121

Seventeen ◆ On Goals, Attitudes & Beliefs 127

Conclusion 131

Recommended Reading 133

"If you would persuade, you must appeal to interest rather than intellect."

—Benjamin Franklin

Introduction

Ever since I can remember, I have been a salesperson. From the time when I was a little girl selling my neighbors the landscaping rocks from my parent's front yard (much to their dismay), to my award-winning run as the top Girl Scout cookie salesgirl in Albuquerque, New Mexico, until the present day.

I've spent my entire lifetime convincing people to buy my products, ideas and most importantly, myself.

When I was in my early twenties, the opportunity of a lifetime literally fell in my lap. I was working as an advertising sales representative for a small company in Dallas, Texas, where I still live. Because the company was not doing as well as I hoped, I decided to attend a local job fair to see what other opportunities were available.

By chance, I was introduced that day to the man who would soon become my new boss. He hired me to represent the nation's leading sales trainer, Tom Hopkins, author of the mega-hit *How to Master the Art of Selling*.

In that position, I was coached in all of Tom's proven techniques, and had the amazing opportunity to put them to the test by selling sales seminars to salespeople all over the United States and Canada. In that incredibly positive and motivational environment, I was encouraged to spend more time working on myself than on my job. The growth I experienced during those years has so positively affected every area of my life, I felt it was time I wrote about some of these life-changing concepts with the hope of helping other people succeed and live the life they truly want to live.

My job was fun and easy. I traveled all over the U.S., visiting salespeople from all industries and walks of life. I offered them a free 45-minute sales training workshop in exchange for them taking time to hear about an upcoming Hopkins seminar coming soon to their area. My goal was to get them to attend the upcoming program. Several who ultimately did attend told me my persuasive abilities changed their life because if not for the seminar, they would not have learned the techniques that allowed them to become financially free. It just doesn't get any better than that!

To have so many people actually tell me what a difference I made in their lives was an incredible feeling—one few people get to experience at such a young age. Since then and throughout my career, that has been one of my primary motivators, and I have tried to work with and for people who allow me to help others in that way.

Traveling to so many interesting places and meeting people in all kinds of companies was a dream job. I am grateful for the opportunity to become intimately familiar with so many kinds of businesses. By doing that, I realized firsthand something Tom was teaching us all along: it doesn't matter what company you are in or what product you are offering, there are certain principles you can apply to selling that will work every time, regardless of the product or service you are selling.

The Internet has opened up our world in ways I think we could hardly have predicted twenty years ago. Because of that, buyers have changed because they have virtually all the information they need available to them at the touch of a finger. Nearly anything you can think of can be yours by just surfing the Internet.

This has changed the face of selling today because consumers have become so sophisticated. I believe that is the primary reason it is so important to learn sales strategies, and also learn how to sell yourself. In this marketplace, it seems people will buy *you* more than they will buy your product. If they can get what they want when they want from who they want, you have to be the most important item on your offering plate.

Through sincerity, willingness to help others and a desire to truly change the lives of those you serve for the better, you can become successful in 21st century selling.

"Those who would give up essential liberty to purchase a little temporary safety deserve neither liberty nor safety."

—*Benjamin Franklin*

Chapter 1
Rejoicing in the
Title of Salesperson

The beautiful thing about being a professional salesperson is that you literally hold the world in your hands. You have complete control over what you do and when you do it. Most importantly, you also control how much money you make. It is the ultimate freedom and the thing I have always loved about this work.

That said, the fact is the word 'sales' is a four-letter word to many people. If you don't believe me, just tell someone you don't know that you are in sales and just watch their reaction!

It is unfortunate that a few can spoil it for the many, but the truth is many folks have a poor opinion of salespeople because there are a lot of unprofessional people out there who give salespeople an all around bad rap. Occasionally, this abreaction will eventually penetrate your shell and cause you to temporarily feel the same. That is something you have to fight against: remember, selling is truly the greatest profession in the world!

Earlier in my career I worked for one of the largest telephone companies in the U.S. as a sales representative for the yellow pages. I was in outside sales and was assigned to renewal of the larger accounts, such as the attorneys with the full page color ads.

Because this was in the days of deregulation, the phone company had a lot of power and could basically do what they wanted. When I called on a client, I would have a copy of the client's account (including their current ad) with me, and I would prepare a larger program with increased visibility to propose to them for the following year.

The hard part was that even if they kept the ad exactly the same, the phone company would raise their rates by three to four percent. Obviously, this infuriated many of my customers, who would practically throw me out on my ear. Of my many jobs in sales, I have to say this one required the thickest skin.

I eventually left the company, as many did, due to burnout. The only thing keeping many people there was the salary/commission structure, which was extremely high compared to that of other sales positions.

In my next job as Public Relations Director for a small power company, I remember thinking the day I was hired, "Thank God, I finally got out of sales! I've gone beyond it!"

The truth was I needed to *get real*, as Dr. Phil would say. Public Relations is just another fancy name for Sales Rep, and in this position I probably sold more than in just about any other position I've held in my entire career.

In fact, I see so many companies these days who give their salespeople fancy titles and give them positions of illusory power in the company, only so they can hide behind the fact that they are indeed salespeople.

I worked for a utility with the second highest rates in the state of Texas, again, before deregulation hit. The customers in our town were furious with the company. It was something I definitely knew how to handle after my phone company experience. My job was both to help people learn how to save money on their bills by providing energy education programs and to talk to local and state politicians about hastening the deregulation process because our company felt that the sooner deregulation happened, the sooner our rates could be lowered.

Though it was not the kind of sales job where I was selling one particular item, it was still selling and it was something that had to be done around the clock. State representative dinners, cocktail parties, and City Council meetings were all part of the daily routine. I have to say it was one of my most enjoyable occupations.

After that, I further renounced the sales profession in my mind by becoming a private practice counselor, helping people with everything from grief recovery to career advice. Again, in my mind, I had 'graduated' from the life of salesperson and I was happy to be beyond it.

The truth is that as a self-employed entrepreneur, I was absolutely 100% responsible for selling for a living – and on straight commission, at that! If I did not sell a session, a book or a speaking engagement, I did not make any money. This is true selling at its best, and I do love it.

Sales 101: Simple Solutions for Sales Success

As I am sure you will do at some point in your career, it's taken me years of going through this process to realize that I really am a sales person, always have been, always will be—and in my opinion, every single person in every walk of life, regardless of what kind of job they have, is selling *something* in order to survive.

Recently, the air conditioner at my house broke and had to be replaced. After considering two companies we knew of, we called a company we had used before for repairs to replace the unit. Our decision on who to work with was one based on emotion and prior company knowledge. A sale was made the minute we made that buying decision.

When the men came out to do the work, the efficiency with which they do their jobs, combined with how they personally treated us, will allow us to again decide to use them. Do these guys think they are salespeople when they come over to climb in my attic? Probably not, but they should.

During the years I spent working for Tom Hopkins, I had the pleasure of working with some of the top companies in the world. I know they were the top because they were the ones willing to invest in sales training and in teaching their employees the value of outstanding customer service and how business can be expanded by using certain skills. During these years, I worked with all sorts of different service companies, including air conditioning companies, whose sales people really understood that every encounter with a customer was an opportunity to make a valuable impression on them.

You are the same way. Regardless of what you are doing in life, you are constantly selling yourself. Every time you apply for a new job, you are selling yourself. Every time you convince your spouse to go to the movie you want, you are selling. There is no way around it, so in the long run, it is good to develop a healthy attitude about it and enjoy the process.

The selling profession has been wonderful to me through the years because it has given me the freedom to come and go as I please and to be graded on my production and productivity levels rather than by what someone else thinks I am worth.

Let's briefly go over some of the benefits you receive through professional selling:

1. **No income limit** – nobody tells you how much or how little you make. It is all up to you!

2. **Freedom and flexibility** – this is huge for me personally. You decide when to hit it hard or when to take a break. You are totally self-reliant.

3. **Creativity** – *you* are really what the customer is buying, especially these days. The conversations you have and presentations you make are all a reflection of your unique style and personality. It is all up to you how to sell it and you get to use your creativity like no other career.

I hope you will also come to embrace the profession of sales and appreciate all the perks and benefits in store for you! There is cause to rejoice! You have found a wonderful career!

Study Questions: Rejoicing in the Title of Salesperson

1. How do you feel about being a salesperson?

_____

_____

_____

_____

_____

_____

2. Do you have a title other than "sales" for your job?

_____

_____

_____

3. Write a list of some of the things you enjoy most about your job and about selling as a profession that were not listed above.

_____

_____

_____

_____

_____

_____

_____

_____

"Energy and persistence conquer all things."
—Benjamin Franklin

Chapter 2
Do What it Takes to Succeed

In any profession you choose, you have to be willing to put in the time and do whatever it takes to be successful.

A favorite story my former boss told his colleagues was about a situation I encountered after I became a Tom Hopkins representative.

We spent most of our time as representatives living in corporate housing in some other city other than our own. Typically, I would leave in January and be gone from home until September when the seminar came through the Dallas, Texas area, where I live.

If you've ever been in Texas in August/September, you know that it is scorching hot there – over 100 degrees nearly every day.

I am a person who really doesn't like to wear shoes, and in the summer I would stop by my house for lunch and to get ready for my afternoon appointments. On hot summer days,

I often took my shoes off and put them behind the seat of my car. On this particular day, however, I took them off in the house and apparently forgot to put them back on.

Seems hard to believe, doesn't it? Unfortunately, I didn't recall this little mishap until I was at the client's office and it was around 3:30, which is when rush hour begins in Dallas. I always arrived at least thirty to forty-five minutes early, and you can imagine my horror at realizing I had no shoes!

Since I was in an industrial area, there were no shops around, and I couldn't risk being late to the meeting by driving off somewhere.

Just then, an incredibly ridiculous thought came to me: I would have to get shoes from someone at the office park. The question was, how?

I got out of my car and started eyeing prospects. I'd walk up to them and say, "Uh, excuse me...I know this is going to sound crazy, but I'm wondering if I could buy your shoes."

I was taught by Hopkins to keep my mouth shut after asking the closing question, so I just stood there, in all the seriousness I could muster up, and waited for the response.

I have to laugh now, but it was not too funny at the time watching the people stare back at me in horror and back up as if I had the plague. This is fashion-conscious Dallas,Texas, after all. I must have looked like a complete imbecile!

I particularly remember one woman's extreme reaction to my request. "Get away from me," she said, as she ran down the sidewalk.

I did not give up on her, though, because I had been sizing up her feet and the shoe color was a great match, so

I kept going. "I could just rent them from you if you'd like...."

I was lucky she didn't call the cops!

Finally, there was a really friendly looking lady who walked out the door just about the time I was set to go to the meeting barefoot. I walked up to her and decided that the rental request may be the best plan. "Excuse me," I said, clutching a twenty dollar bill, "I know this is going to sound crazy, but I am just about late for a meeting and I left my house without my shoes. I am wondering if I could pay you twenty bucks to borrow your shoes – rent them, actually – for about an hour and when I'm done, I'll put them here, behind this potted plant in the lobby."

I don't know if it was the grace of God, how I presented it, my evident complete and utter desperation, or the fact that I had just about given up. But the lady looked slowly to the left, then to the right, and when she was certain nobody was looking, she snatched that twenty out of my hand, kicked her shoes off and ran out the door.

"Thank you, oh, thank you!" I exclaimed, sounding, I'm sure, like a common street beggar.

I threw the shoes on, raced up the elevator, put on an adrenaline-packed performance, and walked out with the whole office signed up to attend the program. I felt wonderful—and I put the shoes behind the plant on the way out the door.

I wound up telling my former boss about this little incident and he still laughs about it to this day whenever I talk to him. Much to my chagrin, he told the man at the company I'd made my presentation to that day what I had done. He thought it was the funniest thing he'd ever heard and wished I would've told them all about it during the meeting! I didn't want them to know, but I suppose when push comes to shove, you sometimes have to throw your dignity out the window to make the sale!

What Goes Around Comes Around

An incredible postscript to that story happened in January 2006—literally fifteen years later—when I was doing my own book signings and seminar in Orlando, Florida.

When I arrived in the airport, a breathless lady rushed up to me and said, "I know this is going to sound crazy, but I was wondering if I could buy your shoes."

I kid you not, I almost passed out! She was completely exasperated because her husband was taking her on a charter flight with a bunch of business executives and she would not be allowed on the flight with her tennis shoes on.

What's even better is that she put $40 in my face and said, "Here, I'll give you $40 and you can have these shoes to wear out of here. They're practically brand new!"

I started to explain to her I had been in this exact situation, but she was too frazzled to listen, so I instantly kicked off my shoes and handed them over, taking the $40 and slipping on the new tennis shoes.

The moral of the story – do what it takes, do your best, and you will eventually be rewarded, even if it takes 15 years!

"He that is of the opinion money will do everything may well be suspected of doing everything for money."

—*Benjamin Franklin*

Chapter 3
The Energy of Money

Once you've decided that being a salesperson is okay, and you develop a stick-to-it attitude, the next thing I've seen people battle with in life in general is what I like to call an unhealthy relationship with or attitude about making money.

For the past several years, I've worked in the field of alternative healing. In that industry in particular, there are lots of folks with the "starving artist" mentality who are "starving," so to speak, because they have a belief that money is bad karma or the old classic, "the root of all evil."

I would like to think I would not even have to mention this here, but through my counseling work and other experience, I've found that there are a lot of people who really do need to hear this: Money is energy! It is not evil! It is the level of energy exchanged for your product or service! It is okay to have lots of energy in the form of money, particularly when it is in direct proportion to the amount of energy you are bringing to the marketplace.

I am a certified hypnotherapist, and in that field, I work with the subconscious minds of individuals, rather than with people as they are in the waking state. Right now you are probably reading this thinking, "This is ridiculous! I know money is okay and I want to make lots of it! Why is she even bothering?"

That is your conscious mind talking, and of course, the last thing any of us wants to admit is that we don't want to strive for the almighty buck. Financial status is a huge part of our culture these days.

An unhealthy obsession with cash is not good either, but in my opinion, a healthy relationship with cash flow is critical to driving the motivation that will lead you to making more sales.

I sometimes find in counseling work that the person is consciously thinking and feeling one thing, but subconsciously there is a limiting belief or idea about money holding them back and preventing the level of success they really want to reach.

In a moment, I would like you to do me a favor and answer the following questions. It is important that when you see these questions you think about the very first thing that pops into your mind without judging it or dismissing it altogether.

Okay? Here goes:

Exercise

1. Money is _____
2. Money is _____
3. Money is _____
4. Money is _____
5. Money is _____

Great! How did you do? Did you attempt to change your answers or not write down what you really think? If so, do this again and just be honest with yourself. Nobody will see this but you.

Several years ago when I did an exercise similar to this, the first thing that came to mind was, "Money is evil." I was shocked, to say the least! Is that because I've been watching too many TV shows or movies with that theme? Who knows, but the bottom line is that as long as I believed that, then I would have a hard time making money. Wouldn't you agree? It was something that needed to be cleared and replaced with a more positive feeling about cash flow.

This is the same thing I find with many of the coaching clients I work with. They also have deep-rooted feelings or limiting beliefs about money and then wonder why they are not as successful as they'd like to be. It's just a matter of changing the input a bit so the output is more in line with what you want to create.

The point of looking at that is not to judge yourself, but to just take the temperature of your relationship with money and see what kind of true beliefs you have about it.

How many of your responses were positive? How many were less than positive? If any of them were less empowering than you'd like, the next step is to begin to replace those thoughts with something more positive.

The next exercise will involve guided imagery, where you will be asked to do some imagining. You can see things, feel them, or just have an inner knowing about them, but it is important for you to consider the first things that come into your mind.

Exercise

In this exercise, I'd like to take you on a guided imagery journey to the place where you created the beliefs that were less than positive, and help you replace these with new ones.

Before we begin, you need to do a few things:

1. Look at the list you created above and circle anything you wrote down that is less than empowering to you and your goals.

2. Write down a new belief to replace the old one. For example, if you said something like "money is bad," think about how you would replace that to make it more powerful for you. You could instead say something like, "Money is energy, and the more energy I have the more I can provide for my family." Take a few moments to write new, powerful responses to your thoughts on money.

3. Now write another statement about how you wish to be with regard to your financial freedom. Write it as if it is already happening. For example, you could say something like, "I am making $_____ per month and I am financially free." Or you could say something like, "My net

Shelley Kaehr, Ph.D.

worth is $_____$ and I am the top producer in my company."

Okay, great! Now that you have answered the questions above, let's go into a little relaxation process that I do with executives to help you in your relationship with money. You may want to record this process and play it back. Your subconscious mind loves the sound of your voice!

Guided Imagery Exercise

Find a comfortable chair and sit down. Close your eyes. Now imagine feeling a wave of relaxation pouring in through the top of your head. Feel it move down through your eyes, your nose, your mouth and jaw, and into your neck. Imagine it washing over you like waves on the ocean and moving down, down, down, into your arms, your elbows, your wrists, hands, fingertips. Very good.

Feel this relaxing sensation move into your back, your shoulder blades, into your heart, down, down, down through your stomach, all the way down to the base of your spine. Imagine it is pouring through you carrying away any tension from today. Very Good!

Now imagine it is moving into your legs – into your knees, ankles and all the way down into the soles of your feet. Imagine this wave is like a waterfall carrying away all tension and allowing it to move down, down, down, and out the soles of your feet and down into the earth.

Imagine it gets stronger and stronger and it begins to pour out your heart, creating a relaxing golden bubble of light that surrounds you by about three feet in all directions.

Very good.

Now imagine this bubble of light begins to lift up, up, up into the air, floating higher and higher and higher, up, up, up…feel yourself just floating away, leaving the world behind as you go higher and higher and higher. Imagine that the higher up you float, the more relaxed you feel. Up, up, up….

As you continue to float higher and higher, you notice you have now floated so high in the sky that as you look down, you notice something that looks or feels like a beam of laser light below you. This laser light represents your lifeline, or the way that you sort time.

Imagine you are gently floating over today, peaceful and relaxed. Now imagine you can turn and look out in the direction of your future and notice how bright your future is.

Imagine you can look into your past, and as you do, it becomes brighter and brighter and brighter. Very good.

In just a moment you are going to float back into your past, to the source event where you made a decision about money that was not in your best interest. The place where you first created the belief you wrote down earlier.

You are still surrounded by this golden peaceful light and when I count to three you will begin to float back to this event where you made a decision about money that is no longer serving you. One, two three…floating back, back, back, very quickly now, and by the time I count to three again you will arrive at this source event. One, floating back, back, back, two, further and further and three…you're there!

Now imagine you can float into this event and notice what is happening. What is the decision you made about money? How is this affecting your prosperity now? Are you ready to let go of this? Great! Imagine the thoughts and feelings that created this decision are letting go and melting away. Imagine you can feel them leaving your body and floating out the soles of your feet. Very good!

What new decision about money would you like to have now that would change everything for the better? Remember what you wrote earlier about money and imagine you can make that new decision right now. Very good.

Now imagine your subconscious mind can give you a visual image or thought that represents the new feeling you have about money. What is that thought or image? It could be a dollar sign, a bird, a butterfly....notice the first thing that comes into your mind. Very good.

I want you to imagine that from now on, anytime you think of that image or see it in the world, you will instantly recall this new feeling and decision you have about making money. Very good!

Now take that feeling and image with you as you float up, up, up, out of that event and slowly begin to come back toward now, noticing how every single thing between then and now is totally realigned and re-evaluated in light of this new decision. Very good.

Now glance out toward your future and notice how much brighter it is now than before. Very good.

Now begin to float back down, down, down, through the clouds, feeling the gravitational forces of earth bringing you back down until once again you land, back where you started, still surrounded by golden light and in just a moment when I count to five, you will come back feeling awake, refreshed and better than you did before.

Five, grounded, centered and balanced, four, continuing to process this information in your dreams tonight so by tomorrow morning you are fully integrated into these new powerful beliefs about money, three, being safe in all activities, two, remembering that any time you think about that special image you will instantly be drawn back into the space where you are empowered and have a wonderful relationship with the energy of money, two, one, grounded, centered and balanced, and BACK! Opening your eyes!

How was that experience? I have found that simple journeys in our imagination like the one above can be very powerful in assisting us in moving forward in life and opening ourselves to increased prosperity and abundance.

Study Questions:
The Energy of Money

1. What did you think of your initial answers to the above questions about money?

_____

_____

_____

_____

_____

2. Were you surprised?

_____

3. What new or more positive attributes can you assign to the energy of money?

_____

_____

_____

4. How did the visualization assist you in shifting your beliefs about money?

_____

_____

_____

_____

_____

_____

_____

"Dost thou love life? Then do not squander time, for that's the stuff life is made of."
—*Benjamin Franklin*

Chapter 4
Get Motivated!

There's a lot of talk in the sales industry about the fact that the key to your success is to just get out there and get motivated.

That is sometimes easier said than done. What makes one person enthusiastically rush out to make sales calls and another barely able to get out of bed in the morning? That's a tough one to answer!

When I was with Tom Hopkins, one of the main things we were taught to do was to listen to positive messages every day through motivational tapes, affirmations and lectures designed to help us create a positive image of the world around us.

When I work with clients in my private practice, I often help them to develop their own form of self-talk and personalized affirmations that help them achieve their goals.

Many people believe that life is hard, you need to work your tail off to get ahead, and that happiness is something reserved for fairy tales and fantasies.

I totally disagree with all of that. Your life is what you make it and there is nothing wrong, in my opinion, with wearing those rose-colored glasses and seeing the positive things the world has to offer, of which there are many.

There is an old saying that you get what you think about, and to me, the more you look on the bright side of things and enjoy the journey, the more you will notice yourself filled with an abundance of energy and enthusiasm about yourself, your life and your products.

What I am talking about here is similar to what we discussed in the last chapter, when we identified your unproductive beliefs around money and replaced them with positive new beliefs called affirmations.

I spent many years studying the field of neuro-linguistic programming. In that modality, the brain is always compared to a computer, meaning input affects output. In other words, whatever is filling your mind is going to affect your outer world. Period.

My first book on selling, *53 Affirmations for Sales Perfectionists*, contained tips on how to make your day the best it can be. Those tips are included in part two of this book.

If you are constantly bombarding yourself with the local news and negativity, then that is what your mind is filled with when you go out to meet customers.

On the other hand, if you choose to fill your mind with positive thoughts, particularly in the morning when you are most impressionable, you will carry that attitude with you throughout the day and you will pass that energy on to everyone who meets you.

When I was with Hopkins, we listened to motivational material literally 24 hours a day, seven days a week, to the exclusion of everything else. It was very helpful during those years for us to do this because it ingrained a certain set of core beliefs deep within our psyche that I know is still helping me today.

As Tom said, 'It takes 21 days to effect a change.' That is true, it does, and by deeply embedding such hopeful and positive information into our minds, we were able to make some absolutely incredible things happen.

That said, I do believe balance is required in this regard. Stay positive, while understanding the world around you is so important.

What I mean by that is that you do need to be positive, listen to good messages and avoid the depressing local newscasts, but on the other side of the coin, if you have no clue what is happening in our world, you will look like an idiot in front of the client.

I think the key here is balance and being well-rounded. The sales profession is very exciting because it puts you in touch with people from all walks of life, with all kinds of backgrounds and beliefs and the more you know a little about a lot, the more you can relate to almost everyone.

I happen to believe the local news is the worst thing in the world for putting negativity into the atmosphere. If you spend your day hearing about drive-by shootings, robberies and murders right in your neighborhood, you'll be reluctant to even leave the house!

For the past several years I have hosted a radio program. In that business, I have had to develop my own means for dealing with the news so I look informed without having it get me down and affect my overall mood.

These days, I prefer to glance at the headlines on the front page of *The Dallas Morning News* every day, which usually refers to national and global events, look at the sports page if there is a big game going on, glance at the front of the business page to see whether there are any big mergers, acquisitions or other things going on I need to be aware of, and read the celebrity trash page, which to me is a huge part of our culture whether we like it or not. This gives me a well rounded view of what is happening in the world and something to talk about to almost anyone I encounter.

The key to it for me is the glancing part. I do not spend too much time absorbed in any particular area unless the story is of real interest to me. Otherwise, a brief look at it serves most of my needs. From time to time I will find an article or news item that is applicable to what I am talking about on my show, and if need be, I can then clip it and refer to it later.

If I have to listen to the news, I like National Public Radio because it is intellectual, well produced and includes a unique variety of stories. Plus, because I've hosted my own talk show for several years, radio is my media outlet of choice. Visual images, particularly negative ones, profoundly impact your psyche where as hearing it has less impact.

If TV is your preference, just turn on CNN or FOX News at the top of any hour and you can get the headlines in just a few minutes without getting too overly involved by it all.

The point I want to make here is that information is flooding your consciousness around the clock. You need to do your due diligence by filtering and being mindful of what you are putting into your mind. It is very important! And within the barrage of media and news, you must make a concentrated effort at ensuring that most of what is being input into your brain is either motivational or uplifting. It is a discipline you must develop and you must make a conscious effort at doing it because, believe me, the media is not taking care of this for you!

Where to gain your positive daily messages? You can get these from a lot of sources. You can:

1. Subscribe to an email list with daily hopeful messages

2. Read from a favorite collection every morning such as *Chicken Soup for the Soul*

3. Listen to audiotapes or CDs in your car on the way to work – I think this is extremely powerful for anyone in business!

4. Pick up your Bible and open to a random passage each morning. You will see how the one you picked speaks to your situation that day. It is powerful!

5. Post signs and notes to yourself on the bathroom mirror you can repeat every morning while you get ready such as "I am a money magnet!" or "I am having a successful day!" Looking yourself in the eye in the mirror is very effective!

Of course, these are just a few thoughts. In the back of the book I will list some resources for you and recommended reading of where you can go to get this kind of information.

Study Questions — Get Motivated!

1. What things do you do to get yourself moving and motivated?

_____

_____

_____

_____

_____

_____

_____

_____

2. What works better for you — reading something or hearing it?

_____

_____

3. What new habit can you begin now to get motivational materials into your life?

_____

_____

_____

_____

_____

_____

_____

_____

Well done is better than well said.
                              —*Benjamin Franklin*

Chapter 5
Do As I Do

In order to get motivated to get out of bed every morning and do any kind of job, I think you need to be passionate about it, and believe in your product or service. In short, you need to walk your walk and talk your talk.

Looking back, I think that is one of the biggest keys to my success is that I have always adopted the policy that I can not convince you to do anything I am not willing to do myself.

It makes sense, right? How can I possibly convince you to part with your hard-earned cash if I am not willing to do the same? In my opinion, that is the only way to be credible.

Granted, this will not be possible in every place you work. The power company I worked for wanted to hire only people who lived right in the town we served. I happened to live north of there, and I did not feel it was necessary to sell my house and move, which they agreed to. But for the most part, when possible, I do my best to have used any product or service I am selling.

In the personal health field there are tons of multi-level companies out there selling all sorts of nutritional supplements and vitamins. One of the primary foundations of their business practice is that the representatives all use the products, tell their friends who tell their friends and so on, and so on... sounds like an old shampoo commercial, doesn't it?

When these representatives are using a product and can personally report on the benefits of how much more energy they have now, or tell you about some health ailment that cleared up as a result of what they were taking, it makes all the difference in whether or not you decide to try it.

I worked for a short time for ADT Security Systems selling residential alarm systems. I immediately had them come out and install a unit in my house so I would be able to tell customers I was using the product and I believed in it. Before taking the position, I was very familiar with the company because I used to work with them on a national level with Tom Hopkins. I not only admired ADT's level of commitment to corporate training, I knew they were the leader in the industry when it came to alarm systems. For all of those reasons and more, I was able to effectively convince others that having a monitored security system was something that not only earned you a homeowners' insurance discount, but also brought great peace of mind. Because there are lots of companies offering this service, it was important for me to believe in ADT, which I did—and it showed.

Think back to some item you purchased in the past year. How did you react to the way the person selling it believed in the product? Did you think to ask the salesperson if he or she used the product themselves? If so, how did that influence your buying decision?

One of the more "in your face" examples of this is women's clothing stores. When you go into any store in a mall or strip center, you will usually see the employees wearing clothing they purchased from that particular store. They are giving you an image as soon as you step through the door of what those clothes will look like on you, or at least your subconscious is picking that up. Usually they only hire young girls who look like models. This speaks to your inner desire to look great, which is exactly what the fashion magazines are all about. They create a longing and a desire within you to look like the person in the magazine.

Personally, I find all that a bit shallow, but the reality is, that is what happens.

So think about this and remember that whenever possible, you need to be using the products you are selling. That way, you can relate to your buyer and know exactly how they feel about the purchase because you share a common experience which brings us to my next point: empathy.

Because buyers are more sophisticated these days, it is more important than ever for you as a salesperson to empathize, or relate, to your customers, meaning you need to genuinely feel for them and their well-being.

People in this country are currently being bombarded by advertising in all areas of their lives: TV, radio, direct mail, the Internet, and every football stadium in the country, just to name a few.

We are also required to take much more personal responsibility for ourselves these days than ever before, as corporations begin to cut benefits and leave investment and insurance decisions up to the individual.

These shifts in our economy and lifestyle make today's buyers very sophisticated and sensitive to garbage when they hear it.

People can tell when you really care versus when you are just trying to make a buck. Because of that, it is important you have your buyer's well-being in mind.

Every once in a while, you will find that although you may feel passionate about your product or service, occasionally there are reasons why it is not in someone's best interests to own what you are offering. Don't get me wrong— these occurrences should be few and far between, or you are not in the right business nor are you representing the product you can truly believe in—but every now and then, you will come face-to-face with an opportunity where you realize it would be easy to talk someone into something but deep down, you know it is not the right thing to do.

This seems so contrary to everything we have been talking about so far. I mean, of course you want to sell something to someone and you want to get everyone you see involved in what you are doing. It's just that once in a great while you will be put to a test of higher standards than most when you can walk away from talking anyone into anything just to pay your bills. In the long run, people will remember when they are treated well and will tell someone about you.

When I used to sell newspaper advertising I had a customer who was really tough to do business with. In fact, everyone was afraid of him. "I don't want to go call on him," one salesperson said.

"Well, I'm not going to do it!" cried another.

"I'll go," I said, while everyone else laughed at me.

"She doesn't know what she's getting into," they said between snickers.

There was no doubt about it; the man was tough. He told tales of all the other sales representatives who had come before and how horrible they all were. I finally realized that it all came down to one thing: listening.

The man had lost his wife, and I really think he just needed someone to listen to him. At the end of my first 'sales call,' when I walked toward the door, he interrupted me. "Hey! Aren't you going to try to sell me something?"

"No, not today," I said. "I'll stop by again next week."

From what he told me, it sounded as if every other salesperson who called on him must have had dollar signs in their eyes. He was intelligent enough to realize they really didn't care whether his business flourished—all they wanted was the sale, at any price.

The next week, I visited this "difficult man" again and learned even more about him. Toward the end of the conversation, I mentioned a special section that we were running in a couple of weeks and walked toward the door, again, not asking him for anything.

On the third visit, a week before the deadline, I went for another visit and he asked me about the special section coming up. Earlier in the conversation he told me something about a new product or way he was doing things, and I realized the special section was not the best place for his ad. "I don't think that would be the best place for you," I said, risking another week with no sale. "I think you'd do better just advertising in the news section like you used to do."

He looked at me and didn't say a word for a few moments. I think he was shocked that I seemed to not care if he spent his money or not, and that I was definitely not interested in it if it was not in his best interests. I'm sure it was something he had not encountered in quite a long time, if ever.

"I suppose if the special section won't work, I'll take a quarter page in the news section then," he said. From that day forward, he became a regular advertiser, to the stunned amazement of everyone in my office.

This is a good example of what I mean here. It is so important for people to trust you and for you to truly have their best interests at heart, regardless of your own desire for commissions and personal gain. In the long run, caring about others and wanting them to be successful will make *you* more successful than you can ever imagine!

Study Questions – Do As I Do

1. How are you currently using your product or service?

_____

_____

_____

_____

_____

2. How can you become more empathetic to your customer's feelings by doing what they do?

_____

_____

_____

_____

3. Are you walking your walk with regard to the product you are selling now? If not, how can you change to incorporate your product in to your life?

_____

_____

_____

_____

_____

_____

Drive thy business or it will drive thee.
                    —Benjamin Franklin

Chapter 6
Product Knowledge

What happens when you are passionate about your product, you treat people fairly and convince only those who you truly believe will benefit from what you have, yet you do not take time to learn everything about your product? Trouble, that's what. It is absolutely critical that you know every single in and out of your product or service, including what it is, how it works, what it does compared to other, similar things out there, and so on. The customer is coming to you and looking to you as the expert in your field. As an expert, you must know all about what you are selling in order to be effective.

When I go to a restaurant, I like to ask my waitperson to tell me which dish is the best on the menu. Normally, if they are any good at all, they can recommend something and nine times out of ten if I order it, the food is wonderful. They have knowledge of the product and because they tried it themselves, they can accurately give a recommendation for it. This is the same in any industry where a sales rep knows his or her product.

Someone I know who works in technical sales recently told me a story about one of his cohorts at work who had never heard of one of the major product lines they sell. Consequently, that associate made a fool of himself in front of a big customer. How confident do you think that client felt with a man who had no idea about an important line of equipment specific to the industry he works in? I would imagine his confidence in that salesperson—and ultimately, that company—went downhill pretty fast after that one. Remember, *you are the company.*

The funniest (and often cited) example of this is, what if you went to the doctor, told him or her what was wrong, and they looked at you blankly and asked you how you would treat it if you were them? It's a silly example, yet it's power- ful as well. I mean how would that make you feel? How confident could you be about a so-called professional who knows nothing about what they are talking about? I would imagine you would run kicking and screaming down the street, or at least you should if you want to stay healthy!

Car dealerships are great example of businesses that do a good job of ensuring their salespeople are knowledgeable about their product. Of course, I realize you may have experienced a nightmare or two while buying a new car—I know I have. But one thing they do right is train the sales- people on the cars they are selling. When you go the lot to test drive a vehicle or simply to ask questions, the sales- people usually have answers.

Another thing they do well was discussed in the last chapter. Normally, car salespeople get a car to drive while they work there or they get to buy one at cost. This helps sales, because they become intimately familiar with how a car handles and all the ins and outs of it. Further, they're setting an example by doing what they would like you to do: drive away in their car. How easy it is for them to recommend a certain model with certain features when they are driving the car themselves.

Of course, life is a learning process and we are not infallible. Everyone is going to run across something they do not know from time to time. That's okay as long as you are willing to admit it and do the research to find the answers. That is part of growing and changing and adapting to meet your customer's needs.

Nobody in the world will fault you for saying the occasional 'I don't know,' then taking time to find the answer and follow-up. It is far better to be completely honest that will pay off big time in the end because you've shown your credibility.

You can always brush up on the various technicalities of your product or service by subscribing to magazines or e-lists for your industry, or reading books on the subject. As mentioned before, though, if you don't like what you are selling, that could be a pretty tedious process. So, make sure what you are selling is something you are actually interested in learning about. Your excitement for the product will rub off on people and make them excited about owning it.

Study Questions –
Product Knowledge

1. How familiar are you with the product you are selling?

_____

_____

_____

_____

_____

2. Do you feel comfortable answering most questions about it?

_____

_____

3.How much do you know about competitors' products?

_____

_____

_____

_____

_____

_____

_____

_____

_____

_____

_____

Glass, china and reputation are easily cracked, and never well mended.

—Benjamin Franklin

Chapter 7
You are Your Company

I talked about this before, but despite the risk of sounding like a broken record, this is, in my opinion, one of the fundamental keys to your success and longevity in sales—or in any profession, for that matter: you must remember that *you* are the physical embodiment of the company where you work. When people see you, they "see" XYZ Company and when they size you up, they are sizing up your entire company almost instantly and making value judgments based on that first impression.

We can go around and around about whether or not it is okay for people to judge each other, but whether or not you like it, that is the way of the world, my friend. Since there is no way around it, it is incredibly important to not only make a super first impression, but to keep that image alive and well in the minds of your customers.

Whether you ever thought about this before, when you go into that car dealership and see that salesperson, that person is the Ford Motor Company, at the deepest subconscious level.

I'm sure at some point in your life you've had a bad experience or two. Let's face it; they happen to the best of us. Can you recall a time when you received horrible service or had a terrible experience with a company that was not resolved to your satisfaction? Did you ever go back to that company ever again? Probably not.

It's one thing when things get messy and the company is doing all they can to remedy the situation. That is wonderful and in that case, you sometimes earn a loyal following for life which is why challenges can often be a salesperson's best friend. When you have a chance to go that extra mile and demonstrate what you are willing and able to do to help someone out, people remember that—*and* they tell their friends!

On the other side of the coin, when a situation is not handled correctly and no effort is made to take care of things, something equally powerful but twice as deadly happens: the disgruntled customers also tell people. They tell everyone and not only are you going to miss out on the opportunity to retain the original customer, you also have no idea what 'poison' is being spread around about you and your company.

One of the most horrific and almost hilarious customer service disasters I ever heard of happened to my mother when she went to buy a car several years ago. It was so bad, I still laugh about it, but I assure you, she still cringes to this day, nearly twenty years later.

She went to a certain name brand dealership to purchase a car for my brother, who is a highly functioning autistic person. He needs reliable transportation with an automatic transmission that is easy for him to use.

Incredibly, when my parents got the car home, they realized that the rear window had no defroster in it – that was not even standard equipment! They took the car back and were told it was 'too late and too bad,' literally.

You don't know my mother, but trust me, she can be hell on wheels when she wants to be! She was infuriated, yet after going around in circles with these morons, there was apparently nothing that could be done. They took the car as is.

About a week after the purchase, my brother was preparing to leave for work and his car wouldn't start. It was dead. My father was out of town at the time, and my mom called the dealership and actually had the thing towed.

When they took a look at it, apparently there was a powerful internal security system installed in the car that needed to be disarmed. Again, my mom was livid at the time and expense this took, the fact she and my dad were never told about any security system, and that she had to take time out of her day to drive my brother to and from work.

When she asked the representative about the hidden system and why she was not told about it, his reply was something our family still gives her a hard time about. He said, "Well, Little Missy, maybe your husband had the alarm installed so you wouldn't be able to leave the house while he was out of town!"

You have to realize we live in Texas, but this really is the most ridiculous example of the Bubba mentality I have ever heard. Now if we really want to rile her up, we just put on our best Texas twang and tell "Little Missy" a thing or two!

It's hard to believe that service could be this bad and that throughout the whole situation, there was never any effort to solve my parents' problems, or even recognition on the part of this particular dealership that my parents were not only displeased, but disgusted.

What happened, as you can imagine, is that my dad and "Little Missy" will never set foot in that company again. I am not just talking about the specific dealership, I am talking about the *brand*.

I'm sure you get what I'm saying here now clearer than ever – when you are representing your company, you are the company. To my parents, that dealership was the corporation itself, so now that company has lost a customer for life.

And you don't want to know how many times that story has passed around our family and friends all over the country.

When you represent your company, you are likely the only face the customer can put on your company. It is fundamentally important to put on your best face and make the most of things. Believe me!

Last year, I signed up for a Citizens' Police Academy in the town where I live. It was a very interesting 13 week course teaching the basics of all our law enforcement people do every day. Talk about everyone being a salesperson: based on what I saw there, law enforcement officials are, in some ways, among the very best.

After the course was over, I joined the citizens' police Alumni Association. On Sundays, we are asked to come into the station when we can and help call warrants. This basically means when someone has an outstanding parking ticket or fine, they are given a warning call before someone comes out to arrest them. It is usually the very last chance before jail time. Sometimes, we have to tell people that if they come within a few feet of the courthouse or the police station that they will be hauled in—pretty interesting stuff, for sure!

When we make these warrant calls, we have to give our name and say we are from the police department. It is important to treat people with courtesy and respect on the phone, andclearly state the details of how they can best take care of the problem.

For those couple of hours, we *are* the police department, because we are the voice on the other end of the line. In this case, they have obviously dealt with the police before; nonetheless, it is important to treat people properly.

I once had an officer tell me when he goes on patrol in neighborhoods, it is almost like a public relations effort because this town is small and crime is rare, but he feels it is his duty to let the people in the neighborhood know he is taking care of them. "It's important for people to see us out here in the community," he said. "That way, they know I'm doing my job and that the money they pay in taxes that is paying my salary is worth it."

This officer epitomizes what we are talking about here, because he is the entire police force when he wears that uniform. He realizes most of us have never met anyone from the police department, and he wants to leave a lasting and positive impact on the customers he serves. Yes, he called them *customers*, which brings me back to what I said in the beginning of the book: I don't care who you are or what your profession is, you are selling yourself and your image 24/7.

Study Questions –
You Are Your Company

1. Had you ever thought of the fact that you are your company before?

_____

2. If you were a prospective client, what would you think of your company based on the way you currently relate to customers?

_____

_____

_____

_____

_____

_____

_____

_____

3. How can you improve what you are currently doing?

_____

_____

_____

_____

_____

_____

_____

_____

"Genius without education is like silver in the mine."

— *Benjamin Franklin*

Eight:
Types of Selling

Although proven techniques can be used regardless of what you are selling, I like to talk to salespeople about the differences between the two main types of selling: tangible and intangible products.

Tangible/Product Driven

About half of all sales are tangible, meaning the product is something you can feel, touch or use. It is normally the way we could describe any physical product sold to the consumer. Examples of this include items such as copy machines, washers and dryers, or cars and trucks.

In this type of selling, the salesperson spends a good portion of his or her time showing off the physical features of the item they are selling. In the car business, the rep shows you the plush interior upholstery, the power steering and the tinted windows. They sell it to you by having you sit in the car and by allowing you to experience the feeling of driving it.

Once you are behind the wheel listening to the stereo, feeling how comfortable the seats are, and how quickly you can get from zero to eighty, the sales rep knows you have become emotionally involved in the tangible product.

As a salesperson, you have to remember that it is not only the object you are selling. You're also selling the emotional response the customer gets from that product: *that* will cause them to want what you are offering.

One technique used by auto salespeople is to get you to take the car home with you for a couple of days to "try it out." Tom Hopkins would call this the *puppy dog close*: once you get that car into your driveway and the first neighbor comes up and says, "Great car!" you have to go buy it to save face.

I recently used the puppy dog close to sell a musical instrument to a client. I'm sure you have probably bought a really expensive item at one time or another that you thought you could never live without, only to find that a few months later it was in the closet or sitting off in a corner of your garage.

The two biggies I think are exercise equipment and musical instruments. In this case, I was gently persuaded to buy a beautiful auto harp several years ago that I played consistently for about a year. I really loved that harp because it was designed so that someone like me, who had no clue what they were doing, could play it and sound like a pro. I found it to be a relaxing way to unwind from the stresses of life, so I bought it.

Recently, a coaching client told me she'd always wanted a harp, so I couldn't resist sending her home with mine. It had been in its case behind my chair for a year and a half.

She was practically flushed as she thanked me profusely and carried it home. The next time I called her I was able to get her credit card number, and the rest is history.

Although the harp, like any other instrument, is a tangible product, what enabled me to sell mine was the benefit of fulfilling this woman's childhood dream, combined with the beauty of the instrument and the wonderfully peaceful sounds it made. That caused my client to feel she could not live without it.

Emotions are what sell, but in tangible sales you use the product's physical features to trigger the emotional response.

Cars and instruments are perhaps easy to become emotional about, but how would you sell a less emotional item, such as a washer and dryer?

You will still show the features of the machine. Lately, there has been a big push on the new front-loading washers that are similar to the ones the laundry mats have used for decades. Supposedly, these are far more energy-efficient and actually get clothes cleaner than the top-loading variety while using less water. Both of these features would appeal to the environmentally conscious buyer, and as a salesperson, that would be the kind of thing you would want to talk about during the sales process. Not only that, but they are smaller, meaning they take up less room and make the laundry room more spacious and tidier than before.

A working mother with a few kids wants to know she won't have to work as hard cleaning the clothes and she will save money on the water bill each month while being able to keep her house cleaner. It is not the physical machine that does that for her, it is the benefit of using that particular brand that makes all the difference.

For a hard-working mother, it is the emotional response of doing less work while having cleaner clothes and saving the planet that makes her want that particular model.

Intangible/Service-Driven

The other type of selling is called intangible. Some people think this is the most difficult type of selling there is. It is the idea-driven sale, or a service where there are no gizmos to look at or features to discuss.

In my career, I've spent the majority of my time selling intangible products. I spent much of my career selling different kinds of advertising from yellow pages to newspaper and radio. I've also sold plenty of tangible items as well, but in my case I prefer to sell ideas and concepts such as advertising.

In advertising, you are selling the idea that the advertising concept will portray the advertiser favorably in the marketplace, thereby bring lots of new business to them, resulting in increased visibility and profits.

You may have heard the story about Burger King and McDonalds. It is commonly told in sales circles about the fact that McDonalds knows they have to keep advertising more than Burger King in order to keep their name in front of the public to a greater extent than their competitor. It would certainly be easy for them to say, "Everyone knows about

Happy Meals and Big Macs, so let's cut our advertising."

The truth is they realize they cannot do that or Burger King would eat them for lunch, so to speak. In order to stay on top, you have to stay in the public eye.

Several years ago, I saw an interview with The Rolling Stones' lead singer, Mick Jagger, on *60 Minutes*. People probably do not realize what a brilliant marketer Jagger is. All of the merchandising and the efforts that go into getting the Stones' name and image out into the public's eye is done very intentionally, and always with the end result in mind.

In that interview, Mick said something I have never forgotten. He said, "I don't care what people are saying about me. As long as they're saying something, I am making money."

Certainly some may not agree with the Hollywood philosophy that 'any press is good press,' but the truth is that even someone as pathetic as a lot of the supermarket tabloid darlings must be making money as long as those tabloids are continuing to talk about them.

So, intangible selling involves the ideas or concepts without any physical product.

Other examples include:

Financial Planning: Here, the customer will purchase from a financial planner if they are convinced that the expertise of that person can help them earn more than they could on their own and if they are even remotely concerned with their financial well being and security for the future. As I mentioned earlier in the book, due to the incredible social shifts over the past decade, more and more people are turning to planners than ever before.

Insurance: Similarly, in insurance sales it is security the customer seeks. The feeling that the loved ones will be provided for should something happen to them is top priority for those who invest in various policies. This product also uses the intangible concept of fear to sell to the public. You may also purchase insurance for fear of an accident or illness. Fear is certainly a powerful motivator that can be used in this industry.

Mortgages: Everyone who owns a home needs one, but here you are selling the reputation of the company—the brand, so to speak—as well as the quality of service and responsiveness and terms or time period for the load and interest rates. Often, this is based solely on interest rates and who can offer the best, but not always. Rates are competitive, so it is the responsibility of the salesperson to become an ally of the prospect and make him or her feel as if you have their best interests in mind.

Electric Utilities: Now that deregulation has occurred, you are likely to choose your service provider based on everything from cost to ethics, if environmental considerations are important to you. Many companies are experimenting with wind power and other forms of alternative fuels, and surveys suggest that Americans are willing to pay more to encourage this experimentation because of the long-term benefits to the planet. All of this is factored into making a decision on who to choose.

Product & Service Driven Sales

There are also products that combine both tangibles and intangibles. A few that come to mind are security sales, cell phone sales and real estate sales.

Security Systems: When I was selling security systems, I had a tangible product to show people, but that was never the focus. Many of the folks who would call in for security systems had heard an ad on TV or looked us up in the phone book. Why? Because they were people who had just been robbed, or whose neighbor's house had just been broken into. What we were selling these people was the peace of mind that would come from knowing that help was just seconds away. It was definitely a fear-based sale.

Cell Phones: These days, phones can have anything from computer games to movie cameras in them, but it is not always these bells and whistles that sell the program. There are so many companies offering the fancy phones that quality of service, the coverage range, the customer service, and the price are all huge factors in deciding which carrier to go with.

Real Estate: Another example of a combo sale is in the home buying market. Of course, in that profession, you are selling a physical house, but it is not the bricks and mortar the buyer is psychologically concerned with; it is the feeling of whether or not this house could become a home. Features such as carpet color or backsplashes in the kitchen are important, but in the end, it is always about how they feel and if they can actually imagine their possessions—and themselves—in that house.

Study Questions – Types of Selling

1. What kind of product are you selling, tangible or intangible?

_____

2. What are some of the features, or physical characteristics, of your product you want to highlight during your sales presentation?

_____

_____

_____

_____

_____

_____

_____

_____

_____

_____

3. What are the benefits to owning your product or service?

_____

_____

_____

_____

_____

"Who is wise?
He that learns from every one.
Who is powerful?
He that governs his passions.
Who is rich? He that is content.
Who is that? Nobody."
—Benjamin Franklin

Chapter 9
Detective Work:
Features and Benefits

As a salesperson, your job is to help the customer or potential client fulfill a need or desire they have. Often, they do not even know they had that desire until you point it out to them. No matter how much we have as human beings, we always want more. That is where you come in. How you become effective at helping people fulfill and identify these unrealized desires is by pointing out the features and more importantly, the benefits, of the product or service you are selling.

If you haven't already, you need to sit down and write out all of the features, or physical attributes, of your product or service – if there are any. That way, you will memorize and internalize this information so when the customer asks you a question, you will be prepared to answer.

You also need to analyze the benefits or outcomes of owning the product or service. Why will people be better off for having what you've got?

You also need to know the difference between these two ideas and realize that ultimately, the customer is buying the benefit they receive from the features. We talked about this before, but I want to reiterate it here.

You have to pretend you are a detective assigned to figure out what this person wants and what they are about. You also have to become a good listener. You have to take an active role in listening to what they want and who they are, and to have genuine concern for their well being. When you get the clues they drop and answers to the carefully thought-out questions you ask, you will be on your way to success!

Features

Features, as I just stated, are the bells and whistles, the physical things that add up to make your product. If you sell microwaves, for example, some have glass turntables, some don't. Some have knobs you turn; others, buttons you push. They also come in different sizes and colors depending on your needs. These are features.

Features can be important because sometimes when customers are going to buy something, they have a set idea in their mind's eye of what that product will look like and what it will be able to do mechanically or physically.

If your customer wants to microwave a turkey, you should not be trying to sell them a mini-unit that only holds a baked potato.

If that sofa needs to be green to match the other furnishings in the house, you are wasting your time and your customer's by showing them the sofa in black, unless you have fabric samples and can get the color they actually want.

Benefits

While features should be taken into some consideration, it is usually the benefits of owning the product or service you offer that drives the customer to you.

Benefits are the end result of having whatever you are selling. It is not only that the microwave can cook the turkey, but it is the ease with which it's cooked – the time and energy your customer saves, the taste of the turkey, prepared in less time than in the oven.

Although the green sofa is important to look at, it had also better be comfortable, if that is what is important, or if aesthetics are more important than comfort, it needs to look good.

Benefits sum up all the great things that the customer believes they will have because they bought your product or service. It is the foundation of selling to understand that they will not buy anything if they cannot see any benefit to it.

Putting It All Together

It is absolutely critical that you understand the difference between a feature and a benefit. When we talked about tangible, or product-driven, sales, there were actual physical features such as color, size, model, brand—everything that describes how that product looks and what exactly it can do: the bells and whistles, so to speak.

Intangibles, as you saw, are more driven by the customer's concept of what they would receive as a result of the ideas or concepts you are presenting to them. It is more exclusively driven by benefits instead of features.

You need to ask questions to determine what is important to your buyer. If you're selling a car, is speed or comfort important? Are racy looks what they're after, or is safety for the family their primary concern? All of these bits of information will help you figure out what is best for them and how to close the sale. We'll cover this more in the chapter on qualifying.

If it is speed they want as a feature, the benefit of that is getting to work faster or impressing their significant other.

If it is looks they are after as a feature, the feeling they get from having a nice car and being the envy of all who know them is of benefit.

If safety is the concern, the features may be that the car has anti-lock brakes and airbags and has performed better in crash tests than other vehicles, and the benefit is knowing the customer can rest assured their family will be safe and secure in that car.

Do you get the idea here? Do you see why the customer is attracted to the feature but makes the buying decision based on the benefits? Great!

Study Questions

1. Describe at least three features of the product you are selling.

_____

_____

_____

_____

_____

_____

_____

2. What are the benefits of owning your product or service? Think of at least three.

_____

_____

_____

_____

3. Think of a product you bought recently. What features did it have that you enjoyed? What were the benefits that helped you decide to buy?

_____

_____

_____

_____

_____

"He that lives upon hope will die fasting."
                                   —*Benjamin Franklin*

Chapter 10
Treasure Hunting: Finding People to Sell

At some point, you have to get out there and hit the streets and find people who are interested in your product or service. One of the biggest mistakes I think people make in sales is sitting around hoping the phone will ring, and thinking that it will all just happen for them without making any real effort. I have news for you, folks; it just doesn't work that way!

If you're lucky, your company is investing in advertising to bring qualified leads to you. By "qualified," I am talking about people with the time, interest and financial resources to invest in your product or service.

If that is the case, then your job becomes much easier, because all you have to do is contact those who have inquired about the product after seeing your ad and begin the questioning process to determine what level of interest they have.

The truth is that kind of thing is the exception, not the rule. Besides, even if the company does give you leads, why would you limit yourself by taking only what is handed to you? You have an unlimited income potential in the sales field if you only make the effort.

Many companies don't advertise or give their representatives any leads, so if you're getting that kind of help from your company, be grateful, but don't become so complacent you won't go out and find people yourself.

In my early days, we used to qualify prospects by giving them a temperature rating: hot, lukewarm or cold.

"Hot" leads would be those who are ready to buy the product now.

"Cold" are those who are curious, but have no compelling interest now or in the future to buy from you.

"Lukewarm" leads are those who have the resources but who, for whatever reason, are unable to proceed now.

It is your job as salesperson to do your best to decide which of these three categories the potential customer is in, then proceed accordingly.

If you were in a personal relationship, for example, at some point I would think you would only be willing to invest the same amount of energy toward that person as they were willing to invest in you. You can tell when someone is interested in you and when they are just passing time by their words and actions. The same is true of your prospects in sales.

You will just know who is really interested in what you are offering by what they say, how they act when you call, if they return your call promptly, and so on. If we were talking about a personal relationship, I would advise you to only spend your time with people who are really interested in you. In the case of sales, I will say the same, with a slight difference: spend the most time with the people who are most interested in you.

The difference is that in a sales or business relationship, just because they aren't interested in you today doesn't mean they won't be ready to purchase something from you in the future. Maybe the timing isn't quite right, so it's important to treat everyone you meet with courtesy and professionalism, and yet don't spend all your time with someone who clearly cannot or will not buy something in the not-so-distant future.

After determining their lead status, you have to develop a strategy for following up with them if that's necessary, letting them go if they aren't interested or closing the sale, which we will talk about in the next chapter.

Follow-up will be discussed again later in the book, but for now I will say that once you determine the person is interested in it and is not wasting your time, you need to develop some kind of what we'd call a 'tickler file' to remind yourself to contact them later.

This could be set up on a 3" x 5" card in a little file you sit on your desk. Blackberrys and other neat computer programs actually allow you to set your computer to tell you when to call them back. Many spit out a report to tell you daily what to do, including who to call back. That's what I call simple!

Of course you wanted to close the sale the first day, but realistically this is not always going to happen. It's important to set up a system for yourself that you will actually use and that's simple to understand.

Just as important is to decide when a lead is cold and when to let this person go so they are not wasting your time or vice versa. There is nothing worse than having someone string you along for days, weeks, months or even years, taking your valuable time and never planning to do business with you. You have nothing but time in life and you want to use it wisely.

I use my intuition to size people up, which is difficult to teach you in a book like this, but I'm sure you have a gut instinct, and you "know when to hold 'em and when to fold 'em," so to speak.

If they seem to be taking me for a ride, so to speak, I may say something direct, such as, "It's okay to tell me you aren't ever going to be interested in this! I can handle it!" Then, I'll laugh a bit like I'm making a joke and wait to see their reaction.

The bottom line is, you don't want to waste their time either. We all only have what we are given. I, for one, want to make the most of what time I have here.

The other reality you may face is having to prospect for leads if your company does not provide them for you. This is tough to do, especially if you are on straight commission as I have been for much of my career. If you like a challenge, though, this type of sales can really get you thinking about creative ways to handle things.

First you need to figure out who your target market really is. What is their age group? What interests do they have? Which magazines or publications are they likely to read, in case you choose to run advertising yourself?

Hopefully, you work in some kind of niche market, where you can hit the majority of people in a few places. I have
been fortunate to be in that situation now and in some of my previous businesses. For example, if I want to do a customized sales training program for your company, I need to call on sales managers in companies with lots of sales-people. That is my niche.

The field of alternative healing is also a niche market. This means there are certain events where I can get a booth to advertise myself, and there are certain publications to advertise in. Even the book distributors are different. This is actually a blessing, because it makes life easy and when I go out to do anything I know it is not a complete shot in the dark.

What you have to do is figure out who your customers are and how you can best reach them. There are many ways to do this, including:

Trade Shows: I have found this to be one of the best because you meet face-to-face with people who are specifi-cally interested in the type of product you are selling. Often, they have to pay to get in, which is even better from a sales perspective: it already says that these are people willing to invest their cash in what you do.

Networking Events: When I worked as a public rela-tions manager, networking was what it was all about. I would go to events from the Chamber of Commerce clubs, to Rotary Club, to networking happy hours. Here you can meet business-minded people from all walks of life who may be interested in your product or service. The good thing is that most of the time, especially at Chambers of Commerce, you are asked to tell a few things about yourself and what you do, and people are open to giving you referrals of people they know who may be interested in your product. Many of these clubs, such as Rotary, are doing great charitable works for the community, and that is always a good thing to participate in!

Advertising: I think this would be a last resort unless you have limited access to the first two options I mentioned, or unless the ad is targeted to people who are specifically geared to what you want to do (in a trade journal, for example). Advertising, although I do believe in it and used to sell it myself, is a less personal way to get your message to people. Of course, you reach lots of folks, but unless you understand the concepts of branding yourself and your company, or unless you or your company are well-known, you'd be better off investing some time pressing the flesh of live prospects. It works for McDonald's because they established themselves as a strong brand. Even if you don't know them personally, so to speak, you feel like you do because you know exactly what to expect every time you go in there. In my hypnotherapy practice, I used to advertise in a local health magazine. While I suppose that got me exposure, it didn't generate a lot of calls. Through time, I have built my business through referrals, and I have met many of the people who have come to see me through the years at live events.

Study Questions: Treasure Hunting

1. How do you go about getting leads?

_____

_____

_____

_____

_____

_____

_____

_____

2. Have you taken time to see which places are generating the most sales for you?

_____

3. What trade shows or networking events could you participate in to increase sales?

_____

_____

_____

_____

_____

_____

_____

_____

_____

_____

"He that can have patience can have what he will."

—*Benjamin Franklin*

Chapter 11
The Pipeline for Success

Time and again, when you work to make new contacts, generate new leads, make more presentations, and close more sales, you will find that your work is varied and interesting. With consistent effort and patience, you can meet and exceed any goal you set for yourself.

The important thing with lead generation is that once you get going with finding interested people, presenting to them, following up, and hopefully closing some sales, you are in the process of filling the so-called "pipeline of sales." Once you do that, you want to keep it full.

You will find you have different people in different stages of development. Some are brand new and you need to call them again in a month; others you talked to a while ago and it's now time to follow up with them again; others are happily filling out your paperwork and are ready to own the product. They will need you to walk them through that process.

It is a kind of juggling act, and you will get paid by the level of skill you display while throwing multiple balls in the air.

You need to sit down and think about your average sale. How long does it take to get them from presentation to closing? A day? A week? A month? Before you move on, get out a piece of paper right now and figure that out.

Based on that, you need to decide how many people who have never talked to you before you need to call each day in order to close enough sales to not only reach, but surpass, your sales quotas.

Take the time to think of this, then put a plan in motion on how you will accomplish your goal. I find it is easiest to structure certain things into my day. You could have the first part of your day—let's say the first hour—devoted to working on paperwork and following up on things from the day before. Then, you could spend a block of time contacting new people, and finally, you could follow up with those you talked to before. You'll have to figure out what makes sense for you.

Of course, life is unpredictable and things may not always work exactly as you planned, but if you can set your intent on attempting to get some structure into your activity, you will be much more productive.

I think one of the biggest challenges facing today's salespeople is the Internet. It is truly both a blessing and a curse! Email can be one of the biggest time wasters in the world, and it is often quite overwhelming.

One of my corporate clients is a company that does lots of advertising in a niche market. They receive tons of follow up via email because thousands of people visit their website daily.

The salespeople should be thrilled they have so many leads, and they are, to some extent. But what ends up happening is they become overwhelmed with all the emails and don't even know where to begin.

With this group, we had to devise a plan of action about what they should be doing each day and how they could get their time management skills up to speed.

I told them about my own way of handling my emails. At the beginning of each day, I always download my new emails and immediately delete the junk mail without even reading it. Normally, that takes about 50 percent of it out of the inbox.

Because you never want to prejudge anyone until you have talked to them first, these representatives were supposed to go ahead and respond to all of their emails with a phone call, rather than with another email that could just get lost in someone else's inbox. They were to call them, preferably at work where they were likely to reach them, and discuss the product with them.

When I met these salespeople, they seemed to have a lot of excuses about why they could not get to all the emails. Again, I realize distractions happen, but the truth is, all they really needed to do is start at the top of the list, pick up the phone, and go for it!

I wanted to be diplomatic, so I showed them how they could go ahead and take the emails in the order in which they were received and to start each day by calling the newest leads. Later in the day was reserved for follow up on older leads, handling paperwork, or dealing with challenges and anything else that needed tending to.

This simple organization of time and properly filling the pipeline allowed the group to instantly increase sales overnight. The month immediately following our training, they had their best month ever! Was any of this rocket science? I hardly think so.

The problem is that sometimes we allow ourselves to become distracted and overwhelmed by looking at the whole thing and saying, "I can't," instead of taking it one step at a time and knowing as long as you are doing the best you can, it will all get done when it gets done. No need to get overwhelmed! Just do it!

Study Questions:
Pipeline for Success

1. How do you structure your day?

_____

_____

_____

_____

_____

_____

_____

_____

2. How many new people do you contact each day about your product or service?

_____

3. How could you organize your time to better fill your pipeline?

_____

_____

_____

_____

_____

_____

_____

_____

_____

"Be civil to all; sociable to many; familiar with few; friend to one; enemy to none."
—Benjamin Franklin

Chapter 12
Qualifying

There are billions of people living in the world, but only certain ones who are willing and able to purchase your product or service. You will find them through a process called "qualification," which helps you to narrow the field step-by-step so you are only working with those who can actually get involved with what you are offering.

I was recently out training a sales organization. They had plenty of people interested in their product, yet their sales were consistently under quota. Something was glaringly wrong. After interviewing the management about what needed to be covered, it became glaringly apparent that the biggest obstacle to the success of the team fell in this category.

We touched on this in Chapter 10 when I discussed how you "take the temperature" to determine who is interested in what you are selling and who isn't. That is the first aspect of the skill of qualification, but the more critical part that we did not cover in that chapter involves your ability to question the potential buyer to uncover what they need and why they need it.

I think I've always had an almost unfair advantage in this arena because I spent so much of my time working as an investigative newspaper reporter and editor-in-chief of my college paper. In this area, you must learn how to question other people about things, or you won't have any material for a story.

I could present a whole one-day program teaching you the importance of asking good questions and why this is paramount to your success in sales. It is, without a doubt, a powerful skill to be able to really get into someone's consciousness and engage them in a meaningful conversation.

I also practice this in my radio program. The format of the show normally involves me reading some famous author's book and interviewing them about it. Why they were prompted to create it in the first place, what the book means to them and the message they want people to leave with are all important facets of fishing this type of information out of someone.

I think the secret to being successful at it is simply giving a damn. I know that sounds a bit harsh, but it's true. First and foremost, you must sincerely care about others, in a spirit that is not solely driven by your own personal needs, but more about the needs of those around you and by being interested in the lives of other people, their motivations and how and why they do things.

In sales, if you want to be successful you will have to get to know the people you serve and really care about them. It is like forging a new friendship, and oftentimes your customers can and will become lifelong friends if you are sincere and treat them properly.

So while I cannot simply wave my wand and make you a fabulous questioner, I can ask that you think about how you go about interacting with new people, in any area of your life. How you get to know others as human beings is exactly the same type of thing you do in qualifying. Once you establish a rapport with people and you earn their trust, then asking the tough questions such as, "Are you the person who is going to make the buying decision?" is really easy to do and just a part of the continual dialogue of open and honest communication you have with the client.

While you are pondering all of that in your world, there are some simple steps you can follow to help guide you through some of the more important questions you will need to ask a potential customer. Just by asking the prospect a few simple questions, you will instantly know if what you are offering is a fit for them. Some important questions include:

1) What do they have now?
2) How long have they been using it?
3) What do they like most about what they have now?
4) What would they change?
5) How do they see your product fitting in to what they are looking for?
6) Who besides themselves will make the decision to buy?
7) If you find what they are looking for, would they be ready to go ahead today?

Now, let's dissect those questions.

1) What do they have now? You, as salesperson, must get to know the customer and build rapport while at the same time gathering information that can be used to help you ultimately close the sale. You want to know what they have now because it tells you a lot about the person. Several things could happen. They may tell you they never had your type of product before, which would suggest you may need to spend a little more time explaining things to them initially. They may say they have a product of your competitor's now. If you have done your homework, you should know all about that competitive product, and so you can structure your presentation to areas where your product may stand above the competitor's, while at the same time highlighting ways the two products are the same. Be careful with this, though. What if you begin to highlight an area that the customer did not like about that last brand? That's why we go into question number three.

2) How long have you been using it? Again, you want to get the history.

3) What did you like most about what you have now? This is where you listen to what is being said so when you begin to tell them about your product you can highlight the things they told you were important.

4) What would you change? Again, this is information you use to highlight why your product meets their needs (assuming it does) and answers their concerns.

5) How do you see our product fitting in with your needs? You can also phrase this as, "What made you decide to consider our brand?" What you are after here is to have them travel into their future, use their imagination, and see themselves owning your product. How they imagine it will fit into their lives is having them assume they already own it. It is a powerful visualization.

6) Who besides you will make the decision? If you don't get this information up front, you wind up telling them all about what you have, only to find in the end that they have to go talk to Uncle Joe about it and there you are, empty-handed. Don't waste your time or theirs until you have gathered everyone who will be involved in the decision process. If they tell you someone who is not there will be helping them, stop and ask for an appointment when all of you can meet.

7) Would you be able to go ahead today? Don't even ask this question if they already told you that Uncle Joe has to be there. You will only be wasting your breath. If they can't do it today, you have to isolate why not or make an appointment for a future date.

Qualifying, to me, is like becoming a private detective. You are a fact finder and you are digging to learn more about the suspect, or buyer.

Remember, though, you must first build the trust and the rapport before you go into firing off the ins and outs of who will be paying for this wonderful purchase. If you don't build that trust first, you are building your relationship on a house of cards and it will not have the foundation to support you. Caring first, qualifying second.

The other thing I found to be helpful if you are keeping notes about prospects is to mentally give the person a rating on a scale of 1-3, one being least interested and three being most interested. You determine this based on what they tell you in this qualification process. Now, don't write this down right in front of the person if you are doing some kind of in-person sales, just make a mental note of it.

This is really the same idea as the hot/warm/cold concept, but for some people I've trained, those more abstract concepts are not as powerful to their mind as simply rating them with a numerical scale.

As I mentioned before, there are three kinds of people: those who will, those who won't, and those in the middle.

You cannot persuade the ones who won't, so don't waste too much of your valuable time and energy on it. Either they are just looking, or the product really is not for them.

Then there are those who will and they will throw their credit cards at you no matter what. Take care of them and be thankful and move on.

Where I believe you make your impact is with the ones who are on the fence, so to speak. They are the middle of the road and could go either way. You have the opportunity through your skills of qualifying and presenting to convince them to go ahead. They are qualified and you must use your sales skills to help them make a decision that's good for them. That is where your influence can really be felt, you are changing lives and you are making an incredible impact so put your energy where you can make a difference and this profession will become the most rewarding thing you have ever done.

"Early to bed and early to rise makes a man healthy, wealthy, and wise."
—*Benjamin Franklin*

Chapter 13
Presentation

Once you've figured out who is willing and able to buy your product or service, all decision makers are present and you have established a decent level of rapport, you can proceed with your presentation.

Normally, your company tells you what and how to present. You have been given certain tools to use in the form of visual aids and you have practiced what to say.

I think the most important thing to remember when presenting is that at some point, you have to be the expert and tell them what they want to buy.

The truth is that most folks can't decide what to have for breakfast in the morning, let alone what to do regarding a big financial investment or other purchasing decision.

You've heard this analogy earlier in the book, but here goes again: if I was a doctor and you came in with symptoms, you expect me to tell you what's wrong, right? Not the other way around! It's the same thing here.

If you have a half dozen products to choose from, you have to determine which one they want, based on the answers you received from the questions you asked them in qualification, and you actually have to be strong and confident enough to tell them that is what they need, but not in a way that is pushy or makes them feel threatened.

When you ask them how they imagine using your product, valuable information can come from that process enabling you to really zone in on which ones they are looking at getting.

Consumers today are very smart. Most know they must do their own research and homework to some degree so they are not bamboozled in the marketplace by crafty salespeople.

I think the trend toward doing your own research has escalated over the past twenty years or so, because we are forced by society to make more decisions on our own than ever before.

I worked in the electric utility business right before the whole industry became deregulated. In the old days, so to speak, the power companies and phone companies were assigned to you based on geography and you were essentially stuck with whoever you wound up with based on your address.

These days, you have hundreds to choose from and the decision-making is in the hands of the consumers who have learned to be much savvier so they aren't misled.

It's the same in the workplace. As more corporations are laying people off, we are forced to now shop for our own insurance as well as study our own financial investments.

The company will no longer guarantee us a safe place to fall after retirement – we must take this issue into our own hands, and that requires great diligence and research.

The point of it all is this: when you ask them to tell you what they imagine getting from your company, chances are better than ever that they have actually done their homework. Use that information to assist them. Sometimes they may be deciding between two models of your brand and if that's the case, then you, the listener, the investigator, will make a recommendation based on what they tell you.

If they are locked in to one particular brand already before they get to you, see if you can find ways to help support the decision they already made.

The only way I would go against that decision is if you can solidly provide information about another one of your products that offers more of what you feel they really need based on talking with them. Otherwise, support their decision and their intelligence to choose and research this on their own.

Your presentation may be something the company taught you to do in a certain way, but you must be listening and watching for buying signs. Know that you do not have to go through every little thing you were taught if it is not applicable to what the customer wants and what they are telling you.

Certainly I was taught by my training at Tom Hopkins to memorize the presentation and to anticipate questions and have prepared my answers in advance. At the same time, you need to not be a robot who only operates through rote memorization. You must be flexible, listen and adapt yourself to what the prospect really needs so they feel heard and respected for their intelligence.

The days are long gone when people blindly walk into any sales situation. Treat the customer with respect and make your presentation an adaptable reflection of that respect.

Study Questions – Presentation

1. Do you have a standard presentation for your product or service?

_____

_____

_____

_____

_____

_____

_____

2. Is it something you have memorized or do you work from a notebook, PowerPoint presentation or some other visual aid?

_____

3. What improvements could you make to your presentation?

_____

_____

_____

_____

_____

_____

_____

_____

_____

"All human situations have their inconveniences. We feel those of the present but neither see nor feel those of the future; and hence we often make troublesome changes without amendment, and frequently for the worse."

—Benjamin Franklin

Chapter 14
Overcoming Obstacles/Objections

The biggest part of selling once you find people who are qualified and truly interested in what you have to offer is overcoming the obstacles, or objections, they have to going ahead with the purchase.

What you may or may not realize is that if people are not raising objections to your product, they will not buy anything from you. Objections are often merely questions people have about the product or service. I have found that when you take these questions too personally and blow them out of proportion, assigning all kinds of hidden meanings to them, you are missing one of the greatest opportunities you will have to close the sale.

Here are some of what I consider to be the "biggies," or the major objections, and the only real things stopping people from buying. Once you learn how to handle these objections, you will be on your way to more sales, guaranteed!

Money

I would say nine times out of ten this is the only reason people do not want to buy. Let's face it, if you were a multimillionaire, you could have anything you want, so of course you would want all kinds of things. But since most people are far from millionaire status, the bottom line is often the bottom line.

Remember that I am assuming you did your job and determined that this person really wants what you have. If they don't, no amount of money in the world would make them want it. But if they are really interested in what you have, how will you get them to make the decision to own the product?

This really boils down to how well you did your job. If the product is something they want and they see the values and benefits of it, they will buy. If they don't buy because of money, perhaps you need to go back to the section on qualifying and see where you went wrong.

If they are not blowing smoke, they really want it and you know they can afford it, then so be it. Otherwise, you may have to help with some creative financing options. If they still say no, you have not uncovered the real issue, or they really are completely unqualified and you have been wasting your time. It's that simple.

Recently, I was with my good friend down in Florida. After raising her three daughters, she decided to go back to work as a real estate agent.

She was very excited one day while I was there, because she was about to sell her third house to a young woman who had never owned a home before.

Shelley Kaehr, Ph.D.

The seller was asking around $150,000 for it, and the buyer offered around $135,000. She felt the buyer was going too low with the offer and told her so, but the buyer insisted on making that offer. When my friend presented it to the seller, of course, it was turned down.

I asked her if she figured out the difference between the mortgage amounts on $135,000 versus $150,000. I was sure that way, she would be able to show the young woman that for just a few more dollars a month, she could enjoy the home she loved so much.

My friend said, "Wow! That's a great idea!" Unfortunately, the agency where she worked had not yet taught her how to figure out a monthly payment at that juncture. She was unable to effectively close the gap between the two and the sale was lost.

That drove me nuts, particularly knowing that Tom Hopkins still holds the all-time record for real estate sales, and indirectly through the years and through his tapes and books, even I, who doesn't know a whole lot about real estate, have some tricks up my sleeve! I was pained my friend lost this sale over something so easily preventable!

That is what I am so passionate about when it comes to teaching these things to people. If you really believe in what you are doing, you owe it to the client to learn techniques to help them make decisions that are good for them! Just think, if my friend could have shown her that only $30 a month was standing in the way of her and her dream home, that young woman could have had her house, and my friend could have had *her* sale!

This is the beauty and the glory of selling. If you have something that you know someone wants, it's a life's dream, the answer to prayer and everything they ever wanted, you need to know you have a mission to help them get it! I feel sad when I think about the lady who did not get her beautiful new house. It's not right!

If you can get this fired up about what you do, you will help a ton of people and become a huge success!

Another client of mine is a higher education institution. Often, prospective students were becoming overwhelmed when the admissions representatives were quoting the high price of tuition. Again, it is a matter of presenting the information in bite-sized pieces that are not overwhelming to the buyer. Instead of a $10,000 degree program, why not say it is only 10 percent down and $200 per month. For less than an average car payment, you can go back to school and complete your lifelong dream of getting an education.

These representatives were not always doing this and the sales figures showed it! Of course you need to be open, honest and direct, but you also don't want to scare people off before they get a chance to potentially reap the benefits of what you have, providing it is good for them and something they need or want.

You as salesperson have to sit down with your pricing sheets and financing plans and figure out how to present this information in a gentle-yet-direct way.

As I said, though, you also do not want to come off like you are not telling them the price. After quoting your $200 per month, some people will want to know the total. In the case of the school, those rates are published and most students read that before they call in. In their case, the prospective student is interested in finding out how they will pay for it if they are accepted. Knowing that the payment plan is interest-free is a big relief for most of them.

Doing Business with Your Competition

The other reason you may be unable to sell your product to someone is if they are already doing business with your competitor. Lots of salespeople immediately assume they should not even try for this business, but if you don't, you're leaving money on the table.

You have no idea whether the person is happy with the service they've been receiving. You may just happen to call on the day they are ready to give up on your competitor! You could offer a better price, better service and better product and have a new customer for life.

I think the biggest reason for switching is not always price. It is service. When people are mistreated, sometimes they are willing to pay a bit more to someone else to be treated better.

A friend was telling me about a sales call he went on recently with a coworker. He knew company they were calling on was doing business with the competition. He walked in and walked out with an order for several thousand dollars. His companion was shocked. "I can't believe you did that!" he said. "I never called on them before because I didn't think they would switch."

That very day was the day when that business owner had had enough of the competitor and was ready for a change. You don't know when that time will come. So as long as you know someone uses products like yours, regardless of whether or not they have them already, you should make a point of putting them on your to do list for sales calls. You just never know when your time has arrived.

You have to be prepared to do what it takes to convince people why your product, service and price cannot be beat. It comes down to your belief in your product and your company, as well as your desire to help people have and do what's best for them.

One last note on this – if you are not getting objections from your potential customer, you are finished! Let me explain.

When someone cares enough to ask questions and give objections, it actually means they are interested enough in it to think about your offer.

I was on a trip to Nepal recently and I was walking down the streets as several vendors rushed up to me trying to get me into their shops. One little man followed me through the streets for a solid hour with some containers of lip balm. He kept saying, "Look Madame! Look! For you I'll give you the very best price!" I kept telling him no and he could not hear it. Finally, I stopped and looked him straight in the eye and told him, "Listen to me. You are a nice person, but I do not care if this is free, I do not want it – at any price!"

He still didn't get it so I repeated it again, "If it was free and you handed it to me now, I would refuse it." In sales, that is just about the worst situation you could be in. It is completely over at that point! Move on!

In the case of this guy, I have to admit I am a softy when it comes to people hustling it up on the streets trying to make a living. I did buy a little statue from him, but it took a while to get him over this lip balm thing. That is an important lesson I think in the power of not only listening, but actually *hearing* what the prospect is saying! Think about it!

The other thing to remember is that if people are not interested in what you have at all, it is not a personal judgment against you. You have to understand that you cannot be all things to all people! Don't waste your time. There are billions of people in the world, and somebody out there wants what you have, believe me!

Time

Another big objection with a lot of people is time. They may want what you have, but particularly if it is a luxury item or a service that actually requires their time, they may ultimately balk at it.

Time is a non-issue in some aspects, although in many industries it becomes important.

This is when I think you, as expert, must reach into your arsenal of past satisfied clientele and recall others who felt the same way they did. Tell the stories of other people who also wanted to make the purchase, but questioned whether or not they would actually take the time to use said item or wondered how they would juggle a full work week, a family and this new, time-consuming item. Talk about how they did it and why they are so happy they decided to do so.

A good example of this would be a boat. Let's say someone comes in to look at the boat you are selling. They already did research and determined the boat you have, is their dream come true. They are capable and willing to make the investment, and all parties are present. Sounds easy, right? But what if the doubt creeps in about how much they will use this gargantuan motorcraft of the waters once the initial novelty wears off? We've all had that happen. We were so excited about something we absolutely had to have it, yet within a couple months of sinking our hard-earned cash into it, the pressures and realities of daily life crept in and we never used it again.

How you overcome this successfully is by telling how others did it. Tell them about your other clients who also had busy lives, and actually set a schedule that they stuck to about when they would use the boat. Maybe it was not every weekend, but every other weekend. Tell them about the friends who they were able to entertain and all the fun they had using the boat.

We all need more enjoyment in our lives, and you can overcome this objection if you get them involved in the fun of it all.

Study Questions – Objections

1. What is the main reason people do not want your product or service?

_____

_____

_____

_____

_____

_____

2. How do you handle that now?

_____

_____

_____

_____

_____

_____

3. How can you incorporate strategies for making people more comfortable with price and service you will provide them?

_____

_____

_____

_____

_____

_____

"*Remember not only to say the right thing in the right place, but far more difficult still, to leave unsaid the wrong thing at the tempting moment.*"

—*Benjamin Franklin*

Chapter 15
Closing: The Art of Asking

The bottom line, as they say, is the bottom line. Regardless of whatever else you're doing, at the end of the day the question is always, "how many sales did you make?"

The first step to closing the sale is to ask for it. I would love to think you realize that already, so forgive me if this is insulting your intelligence in any way. It's just that it is so obvious, it may have somehow slipped through the cracks.

I have to say that asking, although it seems so obvious, is something that strikes genuine fear in the hearts of many a salesperson and I want to make sure you are not one of them.

One of my clients had a sales force that was not very experienced, so they asked me to come do some training to help the few experienced people get back on track and to give what, at the time, were completely new ideas to the newer folks.

There is an old saying that you cannot turn a chicken into an eagle. In this case, they had a wonderful salesperson who was extremely nice, but she was not exactly the outgoing type you would expect to find in such a demanding sales position.

She had been successful in other industries in the past and the sales job was like a second career to her since she was older and reaching retirement age. Like I said, the nicest person in the world, but so mild-mannered!

After going in and taking a look at what was happening, I soon realized that the reason she was struggling was because she never asked for the sale, and there were a couple of reasons for that:

1) Nobody ever told her that is what needed to be done.

2) Part of her felt it was too pushy, and she did not want to be a "pest."

In the training, I covered many ideas with the group about how to close the sale, primarily by just asking for it. I also spent a good deal of time talking about something you and I have discussed throughout this book: if you really believe in what you do (which you should, or you should switch jobs right now), and you feel what you have is helpful to people, then you not only have a job to do, but you have an actual obligation to help people get things that are good for them.

You recall the woman from the previous chapter who did not get to buy her dream home. Granted, I am certain something else came along for her, but the reality is that if the salesperson had known what to do to help her, she would be living at that address right now.

When I put it to her this way—that as a salesperson, she was a helper, a consultant who was helping others—it completely shifted the way she was looking at the job.

I still had to get through some barriers with her about the word "selling." I do not think she enjoyed thinking about herself in that way, particularly since her company called her an "Advisor."

Tom Hopkins spends hours with people teaching them what words to use and what words to avoid, and certainly, as I mentioned in an earlier chapter, there is a very negative connotation for many people about the word sales. Hopkins tells folks not to "sell" anyone anything, but rather to get them "happily involved" with the product or service.

I totally agree with this amazing insight when it comes to dealing with the customer or prospect. The situation here is a bit different because it has more to do with the internal feelings of the salesperson themselves. I believe if you are going to be successful, at some point you have to get yourself in the mindset to accept the fact that your job at the end of the day is to sell something to someone and that there is nothing wrong with that.

Expect to Make the Sale

To the external world, you are an advisor, but to your own inner world you are a salesperson who easily asks people for what you want, which happens to be, in this case, a sale. Ask and you shall receive. You've heard that one before, and believe me, the profession of selling is one of the best ways for you to put this philosophy in to action and actually see the results from that every day.

Many years ago I represented the famous motivational speaker, Jim Rohn, who was Anthony Robbins' mentor. I think he summed it up best when he said that even if you were the lousiest salesperson in the world with absolutely no skills whatsoever, if you ask enough people to buy, eventually someone will say yes.

Even if you said something like, "Ya wouldn't want to buy something, would ya?" someone would eventually say, "I don't know; what are you selling?" and the sale would be made!

It's a numbers game, period. Play the numbers, win the game…eventually. The key is to get so good at the game, the numbers get smaller and smaller and the time between asking and making the sale gets shorter and shorter.

Shut Up

Once you've asked the final question, such as "Would you like to get started today?" or "You can drive off in the car today for only $500 down," the next step to being successful in sales is most critical: shut up.

So many times through the years, I've seen the salesperson become so uncomfortable with the buyer's silence that they continue to ramble on with way too much information.

You may remember my embarrassing story at the beginning of the book about the shoes I rented. When I asked the people to give me the shoes, even then, I had to keep my mouth shut. As I was taught so many years ago, the first person who talks loses.

We are not a society that is at all comfortable with silence, which may be why so many salespeople have trouble with this rule. There is a deep inner strength that comes from feeling comfortable with other people in silence. In any kind of relationship, people often think something is wrong when nobody is talking. In this case, whether it feels uncomfortable or not, you must not let it show. Stay strong, ride it out and wait for the prospect to speak first. Just like asking and receiving helps you build a strong character, asking and shutting up makes you even stronger!

You have to realize that the reason for the silence is probably because the person is mulling what you've said over in his or her mind. They are figuring out how this can fit in their budget, how they feel when they use it, what life would be like with it, and how life would not be the same without it. While these things are being silently pondered in the client's mind, it is important and actually critical you allow them that moment of silence. It's like they are processing things and you need to allow them that space.

Alternate Choice

This book is by no means designed to give you every single technique and how-to there is. If you want to learn numerous closes word for word, which I suggest you do if you're serious about making money in this business, you need to get a copy of Tom Hopkins book, *How to Master the Art of Selling*, which has tons of verbatim closes you can put to use right now. He is the master of that. My book is designed to hopefully give you a few pearls of wisdom from someone who's been out selling for the past 20 plus years, and in that, I am going to tell you what I like the best and what I use the most.

One of the more popular ways to close the sale, and my personal favorite, is the alternate choice close. Let's say you have an item that needs delivery. You simply ask the customer something like, "Would a morning or afternoon delivery be better?" Once they say morning, you continue with, "Tomorrow or Wednesday?" and so on until they own the product.

You can use this technique to pin people down on setting
an appointment, picking out features of a tangible product that eventually lead to the emotional benefits of owning that product, or you can narrow them down to two choices you have so they can feel they are making the decision themselves.

Make the Decision For Them

The next important step to closing is making the customer feel they are in control without giving them too much to think about.

Nobody wants to be told what to do—in fact, people resent that—but on the other side of the coin, if you give someone too much information or too many choices, the brain cannot process it. They will get frustrated and give up entirely.

You are the pro, I hope, and I would like to think that if you have been trained properly. If you are really listening to what the prospect is saying, you will begin to get a clue as to which one or ones of your many products or services would best suit the needs of the person you are talking to.

That is fine if you do, but it is a tender and delicate skill to tell them without telling them. Allow me to explain.

You have to use your brain to narrow down the twenty products to, hopefully, two or no more than three for the customer to choose from. Please do your best to narrow to two because I think you will have greater success that way.

Once you narrow it down in your own mind, you structure what you are presenting to only offer those two things, as if suddenly the rest of it simply disappears.

You will do that by saying something like this: "Mr. Jones, based on what you're telling me about _____ and _____, it looks like either the model A or the model B would be best for you." I'm sure you can see how this is a form of alternate of choice.

Now you have to briefly explain what those are to reiterate what Mr. Jones told you earlier. "Our model A does _____ which would fit in nicely with what you need for your office, and Model B does the same but also has _____ which I think would give you the added benefit of _____."

Based on that last explanation of model A and B, which of the two do you think the salesperson has decided Mr. Jones needs? Model B is the answer. The statement implies that model A is great and model B is the same only with an extra added feature/benefit. Do you see how this works?

It is like you are a doctor, but instead of giving a straight-out diagnosis, you are offering a couple of different treatment options. By doing so, you make the client feel as though he or she is deciding, then they feel empowered to make the decision.

This does not mean you are simply handing them the company catalog and having them point out what they want, you are the pro who is narrowing the field and then you have them select. It is a very powerful operation, and quite effective because everyone wins this way. You are a professional who is fully capable of making a recommendation, yet you are also allowing the customer to have a feeling of personal empowerment, which helps their ego.

These are just a few tips to help you close the sale every time. They are the things I have used consistently over the years, and I hope they help you as they have helped me. I cannot reiterate enough that if you need help closing the sale, practice that skill over and over again and there are lots of great resources I can direct you to in the back of this book to help you get there.

In the case of the shy woman salesperson, it was amazing to me to hear from her manager only two months after our training that she is now the top sales representative in her office. She listened to what she learned in the training and came away from it feeling that it was okay to ask people to get involved with her product. As an "Advisor," after all, she realized her role was to advise, and she did believe in the product.

It goes to show what Hopkins and others have been saying all along: you *can* turn a chicken into an eagle after all, with a little training and willingness on the part of the individual to learn new things and to actually put those things into practice. Incredible!

Study Questions – Closing

1. Which closing technique was most helpful for you?

_____

_____

_____

_____

_____

_____

_____

_____

_____

2. Practice different ways you can ask for the sale.

_____

_____

_____

_____

_____

_____

_____

_____

3. Next time you are in a social situation, practice being quiet for a while and notice how you feel. If you get uncomfortable, stick with it longer and wait for the other person to respond. This is great practice for your real sales situation!

"A good conscience is a continual Christmas."

—*Benjamin Franklin*

Chapter 16
Referrals

This next section involves one of the most powerful and yet underused aspects of selling: the art of getting referrals. Referrals are gifts that keep on giving year after year, and can make all your hard work and efforts pay off in the long run.

You've worked so hard on the sale. Your customer is happy—in fact, they're thrilled—with your product and service and you feel as though you've met a new friend. Wouldn't it make sense for you to ask a happy customer if they have any friends or associates who may be interested in what you have to offer?

Just like asking for the sale itself, though, this sometimes seems like a daunting task to many a salesperson.

I think it is assumed that the only way you can get a referral is if you've been in business a while and you build it up over years of service in the same industry. Certainly I can say after years in counseling that I get 90 percent of my business from referrals, which is wonderful. But even in the initial years of your sales business, you can still get happy customers to tell other people and to tell you who to call on, if you know what you're doing.

Narrowing The Field

This book is not intended to give you every single in and out of sales, but to give you the aspects of important components of the profession that I find most helpful. In the case of referrals, both my own personal experience and what I've gleaned from working with literally thousands of salespeople though the years, tells me that the biggest detriment to success in this area is when the salesperson fails to narrow the field for the customer.

When you ask for referrals, you have to remember to ask properly so you get the answers you want. The problem is that many salespeople are never taught the proper way to ask for a referral.

If you say, "Do you know anyone who might want one of these (products or services)?" your chances of success are slim. Why? Because you have just asked their brain to scan the potential of everyone they have ever met. The category called "anyone" is too big for their mind to get a handle on.

I mentioned earlier that there are some schools of thought, to which I subscribe, that suggest your brain is like a computer. That being the case, if you went into your own PC right now and you wanted to find a document you created a while back, you would go through a series of steps to get there.

First, you would open the Word program; next, you would go into the 'open' command and begin your search. If you simply open the section called, "My Documents," how much success do you think you'll have finding exactly what you need? You have to open that, then go into the particular subject folder. Finally, you will arrive at the specific thing you are looking for—if you can remember where you put it.

If you go through this many steps to get to a letter you wrote a day or two ago, how can you possibly expect your customer to get to a name or two when you have just asked them for the world? It is not possible. You have to narrow it down by finding the "file folder" and then the specific documents, or names of the people, they will tell you.

Exercise

People categorize their friends and acquaintances in files, just like the ones they have on their computers. If you think of it that way, you will be successful.

Let's do a little exercise about thinking of the contacts you have by answering the following:

1) What categories of friends and acquaintances do you have? Think of it in groups such as 'relatives' 'close friends,' 'church,' 'work,' 'school,' etc. Take a moment to list all of the categories you have.

2) Now put the names of at least two people you know in each of the categories you listed. You may think of James from school, Mary from church, and so on.

3) Think about the mental process you just went through to get those names to come to your mind. Can you see now

how your own mind works so you can better understand your customers?

Remember, don't just say "Do you know anybody...?" Instead, ask the customer if they have neighbors who may be interested. Then you'll notice how they begin to think of all the people living near them who may be interested. Next ask if they know anyone at work. Now they begin to think of all their coworkers. Ask if people they go to church with may be interested. Now their mind races to Sunday morning and scans the pews for potential customers.

Study Questions – Referrals

1. How did it feel to you to practice narrowing your own field of contacts?

_____

_____

_____

_____

_____

_____

_____

_____

2. How many steps did it take for you to get to the name of a person you know?

_____

_____

_____

_____

_____

_____

_____

_____

3. Next time you're with a friend, practice asking them about people at work, neighbors, or friends at school and see if you can get them to mention a name or two. Notice how long it took them and also how easy it is to get the information when you ask the right questions and help them narrow the field.

"Do not anticipate trouble, or worry about what may never happen. Keep in the sunlight."

—*Benjamin Franklin*

Chapter 17
On Goals, Attitudes & Beliefs

I've written entire books on this subject alone. The fact is that you are creating your reality with your thoughts. The laws of attraction say that like attracts like, so what you are putting into your head and heart is more than likely what you are getting in the end.

If that is not what you want, you need to take some action to change that. We've talked throughout this book about ways you can guard your most precious commodity as a salesperson—your mind—by filling your head with motivational thoughts and learning new and exciting ways of doing things and creating the life and the career you really want to have.

There is a lot of talk out there about setting goals and I am all for deciding what you want and then writing it down and working toward that.

In my private coaching sessions, one of the things I work with clients most on is this very thing, although I take them through what I call a reverse goal setting. Through this process, they are able to travel out into a possible future via guided imagery and imagine their life the way they truly want it, and in the case of selling, you have to do the same thing.

There are important steps you need to follow:

1. What do you want to create? Is it a six-figure income, a sale to a certain person, a positive meeting with a contact, something else? Whether you realize it or not, you are creating every waking moment, so stop and think about where you are now and where you want to be or what you want to do.

2. Start with the present and go from there. If you have a big meeting with someone this afternoon, I want you to start using your imagination to think about how you want that session to go. What outcome do you want? How can you imagine that the things the person says to you are what you want to happen? It is all possible!

3. Once you've gone over this in your imagination, or in your mind if you will, let it go and allow it to happen. Don't panic or worry about it. Just know that the things you think about create your reality and develop an expectation that you will have what you want. Settle for nothing less than the very best.

If you don't think you know how to do what I am asking here, I want you to do something right now. Imagine yourself at lunch tomorrow. Where will you be? What will you be doing?

I would imagine you either saw an image in your mind's eye of that business luncheon, or the restaurant where you are going to meet some colleagues, or something else. Perhaps you heard yourself telling you what you will be doing or you had an inner feeling about it.

That is the same thing as what I am asking you to do with regard to all your encounters in sales. You have to imagine what you want to happen at the highest potential and then just wait and see how excited you will be when it happens!

When you are at lunch tomorrow, I want you to stop to think and remember what you just noticed about that lunch time. Was it exactly as you imagined? I would bet it will be because that is amongst the laws of the universe and the laws of attraction – *you get what you think about.* So monitor your thoughts, create and think of what you want and your life will be peaceful bliss! I am certain of it!

You have unlimited potential to do, be and have anything you want in this world. Just use your imagination, believe in yourself and watch what happens!

"Hide not your talents, they for use were made. What's a sun-dial in the shade?"
—Benjamin Franklin

Conclusion

Selling has provided me such an interesting and rich life that I am always grateful I got into this kind of work. The feeling of knowing that you are self-reliant and can survive no matter what based on your mental skills and ability to close sales has given me a feeling of deep peace and satisfaction I can hardly imagine would be available in any other kind of vocation. I hope this book offers you ideas and inspirations you can use today to make your selling career a success.

I don't know at what stage of your career this book has found you, but regardless of whether you've been in sales for years, or you are brand new, simply shifting your perspective on things a bit and using some new strategies, or reintegrating old ideas back into your daily routine, can help get you into a state where anything is possible.

Notice I said *using* – not learning. It is one thing to learn and learn, to attend the classes and read the books. That is all great and wonderful, and certainly if you learned something from the writing I will be happy, but to be really successful you need to actually *use* the things you are learning.

There is an old philosophy that I subscribe to and that's this: if from every experience, book, seminar, film, and chance encounter, you walk away with just *one thing* that you can use to make your life better or to bring greater joy to yourself, then that time was well spent.

If I could persuade you to take one idea from this book and actually implement it into your daily activities to make a real improvement in your life, then my work here would be a success.

I hope that this book has provided some of that for you and that you can and will use this material to help make your life more abundant. May you have joy and peace on your path and enjoy the wonderful career you've chosen in selling.

Recommended Reading

Canfield, Jack. *The Success Principles: How to Get from Where You Are to Where You Want to Be*

Chopra, Deepak. *Creating Affluence*

Chopra, Deepak. *The Seven Spiritual Laws of Success*

Clason, George S. *The Richest Man in Babylon*

Dawson, Roger. *Secrets of Power Negotiating*

Eker, T. Harv. *Secrets of the Millionaire Mind: Mastering the Inner Game of Wealth*

Eker, T. Harv. *Speedwealth: How to Make a Million In Your Own Business in 3 Years or Less.*

Girard, Joe. *How to Close Every Sale*

Hill, Napoleon. *Think and Grow Rich*

Hopkins, Tom. *How to Master the Art of Selling*

MacKay, Harvey. *Swim with the Sharks Without Being Eaten Alive*

McGraw, Phil. *Self Matters: Creating Your Life From the Inside Out*

Robbins, Tony. *Unlimited Power*

Rohn, Jim. *Seven Major Pieces of the Life Puzzle*

Rohn, Jim. *Take Charge of Your Life*

Trump, Donald. *How to Get Rich*

Ziglar, Zig. *Secrets of Closing the Sale*

I highly recommend you subscribe to Nightengale-Conant Corporation where you get lots of motivational audio CD programs you can listen to in your car on the way to work! Learn in the car! Motivate yourself in the car! Visit www.nightengale.com today!

Sales 101: Simple Solutions for Sales Success

About the Author

Shelley Kaehr has worked in the field
of human potential for over 20 years.
A former trainer for Tom Hopkins,
she lives near Dallas, Texas.

Visit Shelley online: www.shelleykaehr.com